DRAMA CLASSICS

The Drama Classics series aims to offer the world's greatest plays in affordable paperback editions for students, actors and theatregoers. The hallmarks of the series are accessible introductions, uncluttered texts and an overall theatrical perspective.

Given that readers may be encountering a particular play for the first time, the introduction seeks to fill in the theatrical/historical background and to outline the chief themes rather than concentrate on interpretational and textual analysis. Similarly the play-texts themselves are free of footnotes and other interpolations: instead there is an end-glossary of 'difficult' words and phrases.

The texts of the English-language plays in the series have been prepared taking full account of all existing scholarship. The foreign-language plays have been newly translated into a modern English that is both actable and accurate: many of the translators regularly have their work staged professiona'~

Edited until his ea      ding a
Drama Classics se   he best
first-class library c   D1331736   of world theatre.

Associate editors:

Professor Trevor R. Griffiths

Visiting Professor in Humanities, Universities of Exeter and Hertfordshire

Dr Colin Counsell

School of H
Lo

DRAMA CLASSICS *the first hundred*

*The publishers welcome
suggestions for further titles*

DRAMA CLASSICS

YERMA

by

Federico García Lorca

translated and introduced by
Jo Clifford

NICK HERN BOOKS
London

www.nickhernbooks.co.uk

A Drama Classic

Yerma first published in Great Britain in this translation as a paperback original in 2010 by Nick Hern Books Limited, 14 Larden Road, London W3 7ST

Copyright in the introduction © 2010 Nick Hern Books Ltd

Copyright in this translation © 2010 Jo Clifford

Jo Clifford has asserted her right to be identified as the translator of this work

Typeset by Country Setting, Kingsdown, Kent CT14 8ES
Printed and bound in Great Britain by CPI Bookmarque, Croydon, Surrey

A CIP catalogue record for this book is available from the British Library

ISBN   978 1 85459 578 2

Introduction

Federico García Lorca (1898–1936)

Lorca was born on 5 June 1898. The year was a hugely significant one in Spanish cultural and political history: it gave its name to a whole generation of writers who used the events of this year as a rallying cry in efforts to convince the Spanish people of their country's deplorable state and the desperate need for re-evaluation and change. They were called the 'Generation of '98', and they included Azorín, Baroja and Ángel Ganivet.

The historical event that inspired this movement was the disastrous war with the United States which led to the loss of Cuba, Spain's last remaining colony. This apparently distant event was to have huge repercussions for Lorca. Cuba had been Spain's principal source of sugar; Lorca's father was to be astute enough to plant his land with sugar beet, and with the aid of a series of successful land purchases, he was to become one of the richest men in the Fuente Vaqueros district.

A long-term consequence of this was that Lorca himself never needed to earn his own living. There's no question this wealthy background contributed both to the large volume, and the technical and emotional daring of his work. As it happened, *Blood Wedding* in particular was hugely successful; but the financial security of his position left him absolutely free to write as he wanted, without regard to the demands of the commercial theatre of his day.

However, the most immediate consequence for the young Lorca was that he spent his childhood as the rich son of the wealthiest landowner of a mainly poor village.

Perhaps the best way for us to imagine the impact on Lorca's sensibility is to think of our own feelings towards the desperately poor of the Third World – or the homeless that many of us pass each day on the street. The contrast between his wealth and the poverty of so many of those around him left a deep impression on Lorca, which he was to express in later life in his autobiographical essay 'My Village'.

The plight of one family affected Lorca particularly deeply. One of his friends in the village was a little girl whose father was a chronically ill day-labourer and whose mother was the exhausted victim of countless pregnancies. The one day on which Federico was not allowed to visit their home was washing day: the members of this family had only one set of clothes, and they had to stay inside their house while their only clothes were being washed and dried. Lorca wrote:

> When I returned home on those occasions, I would look into the wardrobe, full of clean, fragrant clothes, and feel dreadfully anxious, with a dead weight on my heart.

He grew up with a profound sense of indignation at this kind of injustice:

> No one dares to ask for what he needs. No one dares . . . to demand bread. And I who say this grew up among these thwarted lives. I protest against this mistreatment of those who work the land.

The young man who wrote this protest at the end of his adolescence maintained a profound anger right to the end of his life. In an interview he gave in 1936, he stated: 'As long as there is economic injustice in the world, the world will be unable to think clearly.'

He continued the interview with a fable to illustrate the difficulties of creating valid art in a situation of economic injustice:

> Two men are walking along a riverbank. One of them is rich, the other poor. One has a full belly and the other fouls the air with his yawns. And the rich man says: 'What a lovely little boat out on the water! Look at that lily blooming on the bank!' And the poor man wails: 'I'm hungry, so hungry!' Of course. The day when hunger is eradicated there is going to be the greatest spiritual explosion the world has ever seen. I'm talking like a real socialist, aren't I?

For Lorca, the art of creating theatre was totally bound up with the process of creating a better society:

> The idea of art for art's sake is something that would be cruel if it weren't, fortunately, so ridiculous. No decent person believes any longer in all that nonsense about pure art, art for art's sake. At this dramatic moment in time, the artist should laugh and cry with his people. We must put down the bouquet of lilies and bury ourselves up to the waist in mud to help those who are looking for lilies. For myself, I have a genuine need to communicate with others. That's why I knocked at the door of the theatre and why I now devote all my talents to it.

This passionate anger at the injustice of human society, and equally passionate determination to create art that might remedy it, were fuelled not simply by his childhood experiences. As an adult, he had travelled to New York, and witnessed at first hand the devastating impact of the Wall Street Crash:

> It's the spectacle of all the world's money in all its splendour, its mad abandon and its cruelty . . . This is where I have got a clear idea of what a huge mass of people fighting to make money is really like. The truth is that it's an international war with just a thin veneer of courtesy . . . We ate breakfast on a thirty-second floor with the head of a bank, a charming person with a cold and feline side quite English. People came in there after being paid. They were all counting dollars. Their hands all had the characteristic tremble that holding money gives them . . . Colin [an acquaintance] had five dollars in his purse and I three. Despite this he said to me: 'We're surrounded by millions and yet the only two decent people here are you and I.'

And when he writes so angrily of the 'thwarted lives' of those whose existence is dominated by money, it is clear Lorca is thinking not simply of the plight of the rural poor, but also of the bourgeoisie to which he himself, and many of us, now belong.

He is concerned not simply with the suffering that a wealthy middle class inflicts on those beneath them on the social scale; he is equally concerned with the suffering they inflict upon themselves. The 'thwarted lives' he saw in his village are not simply those of the poor.

And Lorca reflected this very clearly in *Yerma*: for the comparative wealth possessed by the families involved in the wedding contract brings them no happiness. All the main characters in the play seem trapped by the conventions and the demands of the society they inhabit.

Yerma: **What Happens in the Play**

Act One Scene One   Yerma is dreaming. Someone is singing a lullaby: a shepherd leads a child to her by the hand.

She wakes to the childless reality of the real morning. Her husband Juan is going out to work in the fields. It quickly becomes clear that her desire for a child is at odds with his desire for money. He leaves her in sadness.

Maria, a young woman who has recently got married, comes in, full of excitement. She has just discovered she is pregnant. Her joy deepens Yerma's sense of longing.

Yerma has agreed to sew some baby clothes for Maria. When Victor enters and sees her sewing, he assumes it is because she has become pregnant, and congratulates her. We understand from the way they are together that they have desired each other for many years, and have been forced to repress this desire.

Act One Scene Two   Yerma is on her way back from taking her husband his food in the fields. The first person she meets is an old woman totally in touch with the earth. Yerma asks her for advice. The old woman asks if there is real desire between her and her husband. It becomes clear Yerma has married – and remains with – her husband out of duty.

The old woman seems to sense the hopelessness of Yerma's position and leaves her without giving the advice Yerma asks for. Then Yerma meets two young women. One has left her baby alone in the house; Yerma instils her with fear for her child's welfare.

The other is a rebel who is glad not to have children and utterly rejects the traditional values Yerma so unquestioningly follows.

Then she encounters Victor, and is profoundly moved by his song. Profound erotic currents rise to the surface as they speak; but Juan's arrival interrupts them.

Juan tells Yerma he is spending the night in the fields because it is his turn to receive the water for irrigation. His farm is clearly more important to him than she is, and the act ends with her left alone, rejected and angry.

Act Two Scene One   The village women have been washing their clothes in a stream. They are a kind of Chorus whose individual voices comment on Yerma's situation and judge her in it.

We learn her behaviour is beginning to cause scandal in the village and that Juan has brought in his two sisters to watch over her.

Gossip is cut short by the arrival of the two women themselves. The flocks of sheep are being gathered together: they are like an army. But one person's flock is missing: Victor's.

The women break into a lyrical song of motherhood, and the joy a new child can bring into the world.

Act Two Scene Two   Juan is at home with his two sisters. Yerma is out getting water. Juan is angry that his sisters have let her out; he wants her kept in. When Yerma returns home, he reproaches her for her continuing unhappiness. She reproaches him, even if indirectly, for their lack of children. He goes in to eat; she remains on stage, and lyrically expresses her longing for fulfilment as a wife and a mother.

Maria comes in with her child. Yerma holds him; sees he has the same eyes as his mother, and weeps.

The rebellious young woman of the first act comes in to tell Yerma that her mother, the local wise woman and witch, is ready to take her to the graveyard tonight to perform a magic ceremony that will give her a child.

Victor enters. He and his family are leaving the village, and he has come in to bid Juan and Yerma farewell. Juan has bought Victor's herd; Juan's affairs are prospering, but his and Yerma's emotional life is clearly sterile.

When the two men have gone, Yerma slips out with the young woman to go to the house of her mother the witch.

Juan's two sisters come onto the stage in the gathering darkness to look for her. As they call after her, for the first time we hear her name spoken out loud: Yerma!

It is crucial the audience understand what the name means: barren, sterile – a word for wasteland.

Act Three Scene One Yerma is in the house of Dolores, the witch, after performing the fertility ritual in the graveyard. Dolores is impressed by the courage Yerma has shown, tells her the ritualistic prayers she must repeat, and assures her she will have a child.

Yerma is desperate: aware of the frigidity of her husband, but trapped by the demands of her conventional values. Dawn is beginning to break, but it's as if she cannot bear to return to her emotionally cold home.

Juan and his sisters burst into the house, having been out looking for her. Juan, too, is desperate. The situation is becoming intolerable for him. Yerma fiercely defends her integrity and faithfulness. She tries to come close to him, but he rejects her. She curses him at the top of her voice. Juan insists she keeps quiet to maintain decorum. She seems to submit and quietly returns with him to their house, which for her is now a prison.

Final Scene   Women are gathering for a pilgrimage to the shrine of a supposedly miracle-working saint, whose effigy apparently has the powers to make women fertile. Among them is the pagan old woman of the first act, who takes the rather more cynical, if realistic, view that the whole pilgrimage also attracts men and provides the opportunity for sexual encounters between them and the women. It's this that makes the women fertile; and it's this that is strongly suggested by the explicit dance between two masked figures representing the male and the female.

Yerma encounters the old woman, who tells her very plainly that it's her husband who is to blame for her infertility, and offers her the chance to go with her son instead. Yerma refuses. She is still bound by the demands of her honour, and the old woman loses all sympathy for her and abandons her to her fate.

It turns out Juan has been listening. Their utter incompatibility becomes brutally clear. He tells her he does not ever want a child, but he wants to be reconciled to her. He asks her to kiss him: in her fury and disgust, Yerma kills him. She shouts out to the other pilgrims that she has killed her husband, and she has also killed her hopes of a child.

Lorca and Theatre

Lorca once said that you could judge the health of a nation's culture by looking at the state of its theatre. And for him theatre was a natural extension of poetry: a poetry that leaps off the printed page, escapes from between the pages of books 'and becomes human. It shouts and speaks. It cries and despairs.'

For Lorca there was nothing precious about poetry; it was simply part of living. He once wrote: 'Poetry is something that just walks along the street.'

Because for him it was a part of living, to be deprived of it was a kind of torment; and to deprive people of the chance of experiencing it was a kind of crime. In an interview he gave to an English journalist he spoke of his anger at the lack of theatre that was the norm in Spain outside the capital: 'Theatre is almost dead outside Madrid, and the people suffer accordingly, as they would if they had lost eyes or ears or sense of taste.'

He also said, 'I will always be on the side of those who have nothing.' He was a political writer in the deepest sense, in that the act of writing was part of the struggle for a better world.

Sometimes, when I think of what is going on in the world, I wonder why am I writing? The answer is that

one simply has to work. Work and go on working. Work
and help everyone who deserves it. Work even though at
times it feels like so much wasted effort. Work as a form
of protest. For one's impulse has to be to cry out every
day one wakes up and is confronted by misery and
injustice of every kind: I protest! I protest! I protest!

All these concerns came together in Lorca's work for La
Barraca, the travelling theatre he helped to found in the
early years of the Republic. They would set up a simple
stage in the town square and perform the great, and then
almost completely neglected, classics of the Spanish theatre –
the works of Lope de Vega, Tirso de Molina and Calderón.

His work on this incredibly bold and imaginative precursor
of our own small-scale touring companies had a profound
effect on Lorca. Experiencing the impact these classics made
on a mass audience was a source of strength and
inspiration; and working on the texts themselves must surely
have deepened his remarkable playwriting skills.

In *Blood Wedding*, Lorca began to use these newly acquired
skills to devastating effect. Its electrifying success gave him
the confidence to explore in *Yerma* many of his profoundest
concerns in a new kind of way.

Title

'Yerma' is a proper name that Lorca invented. He created it
through giving the feminine ending to the Spanish word
'yermo', which is a word which describes wasteland, barren
ground, land without cultivation, land which can never bear
harvest or fruit.

Lorca took great care not to have anyone address Yerma directly by name until the end of Act Two in order to give it the strongest possible dramatic impact. Particularly because Yerma is not actually a woman's name, the first audiences would have been acutely aware of its meaning and its power. Which is why it is particularly important that an English-speaking audience doesn't just respond to the word as if it were a woman's name without understanding its meaning and significance. For that reason I have not followed the usual practice of leaving the word untranslated in the title. The audience needs to understand it. This is all the more important because, far more than in any other Lorca play, Yerma herself is the absolute centre of the play. Even on those rare occasions she is physically absent from the stage, she and her situation are always the central focus of the dialogue.

It is significant that, in his subtitle, Lorca does not describe *Yerma* as a play. Instead he calls it: 'A Tragic Poem in Three Acts and Six Scenes'. And one could argue that it barely functions as a play at all. There is an absolute minimum of plot. There is little, if any, character development. What we have instead is an isolated individual in an appalling situation from which she is both unwilling and unable to escape. The noose slowly tightens about her, until in the end she condemns herself to the utter sterility that has, in effect, been hers since the very beginning. In fact in all kinds of ways it shouldn't work as a play at all. The fact that it does work has, I think, to be due to the extraordinary intensity of Lorca's writing and his total empathy with his protagonist.

Sources

In his very touching memoir of his brother, Francisco García Lorca describes how their father used to keep a portrait of his childless first wife, Matilde Palacios, in their childhood home. Lorca himself wrote that his childhood was 'an obsession with certain silver place settings and with portraits of the woman who might have been my mother'. He also mentions the annual pilgrimage to Moclín, where every year there was a procession of childless women to the little hermitage on the hill where the 'True Effigy of the Most Holy Christ of the Cloth' was claimed to grant the miraculous gift of fertility to the childless.

There was a lithograph of the effigy in their country house which Lorca used to contemplate and remark upon. And every year the procession would pass through their village on the way to the shrine, greeted by the derisive shouts of 'Cuckolds!' – aimed at the husbands of the childless women – that grew from the rumours about the rather more down-to-earth explanation of the miracle.

In perhaps less direct ways, too, we can see that Lorca drew inspiration in this play, as in all his others, from the events and social structures that shaped his own life.

Nature and Folk Culture

In *Yerma*, as in *Blood Wedding*, Lorca paints a bleak picture of rural life. But there are moments in the play when we catch glimpses of a very different view of the countryside: when the washerwomen sing a kind of paean of praise to fertility,

and when Yerma herself registers the astonishing beauty
and fecundity of the countryside – a vision of fertility from
which she feels so utterly and desperately excluded.

This is actually far more like the world Lorca mostly saw as
a child. The love of it always remained with him, and, as he
said himself, the natural world remained a source of
inspiration throughout his life:

> I love the countryside. I feel myself linked to it in all my
> emotions. My oldest childhood memories have the
> flavour of the earth. The meadows, the fields, have done
> wonders for me. The wild animals of the countryside, the
> livestock, the people living on the land, all these have a
> fascination very few people grasp. I recall them now
> exactly as I knew them in my childhood.

A still more important source of inspiration was the speech
of the villagers:

> My whole childhood was centred on the village. Shepherds,
> fields, sky, solitude. Total simplicity. I'm often surprised
> when people think that the things in my work are daring
> improvisations of my own, a poet's audacities. Not at all.
> They're authentic details, and seem strange to a lot of
> people because it's not often that we approach life in such
> a simple, straightforward fashion: looking and listening.
> Such an easy thing, isn't it? . . . I have a huge storehouse
> of childhood recollections in which I can hear the people
> speaking. This is poetic memory, and I trust it implicitly.

'This is poetic memory': here we have another key to Lorca's
creativity. As he said himself, he had in his memory a huge
'storehouse' of snatches of folklore, popular expressions and

popular song: a storehouse he could draw on whenever necessary to produce a dazzling array of extraordinary imagery.

This is something denied to most of us, growing up in this age, this place, and this time. The industrial revolution has almost completely erased our folk heritage, and severed our connections with it. In Scotland, where I live, this process was deliberately begun by the destruction of the clan culture following the collapse of the Jacobite rebellion in 1745. In England, where I grew up, the process was less brutal but perhaps more thorough; and folk culture, if it still lives at all, is mostly preserved in museums or in those festivals in which middle-aged people rather self-consciously dress up as Morris dancers, clog dancers, or dancers round the maypole.

Because we have never known it, it is hard for us to appreciate what this folk culture meant, or even measure exactly what it is we have lost. Lorca's biographer, Ian Gibson, expresses it beautifully:

> Lorca inherited all the vigour of a speech that springs from the earth and expresses itself with extraordinary spontaneity. Indeed, one has only to hear the inhabitants of the Vega talk and observe their colourful use of imagery to realise that the metaphorical language of Lorca's theatre and poetry, which seems . . . so original, is rooted in an ancient, collective awareness of nature in which all things – trees, horses, mountains, the moon and the sun, rivers, flowers, human beings – are closely related and interdependent.

Those of us who live in Scotland are fortunate in that to a certain extent spoken Scots still retains some of its vivid capacity for metaphor, its sense of shared culture, its vibrant energy and sense of utter delight in the richness of the spoken word – characteristics that have been beautifully exploited in plays like Tony Roper's *The Steamie* or Liz Lochhead's *Mary Queen of Scots Got Her Head Chopped Off.*

To get a proper sense of Lorca's work, it is most important to reflect on this linguistic richness (which rarely, if ever, comes across in translation), and particularly to reflect on the way in which we all employ and enjoy the use of metaphors – 'black affronted', 'you tube', or 'a load of mince'. It is sad but necessary to add, though, that this is all pretty poor stuff compared to the immense linguistic richness Lorca had at his disposal, and which shines through all his poetry and his plays.

In a celebrated lecture Lorca gave on imagery in the work of the seventeenth-century poet Gongora, he spoke of the connections between this poet's supposedly highly artificial and obscure use of imagery and the completely spontaneous and unaffected use of imagery of the people of Andalucia. For instance, where he came from, Lorca explained, when people want to describe water flowing strongly and slowly along a deep irrigation channel they talk of the 'ox of the water' – a surprising and beautiful image that encapsulates the water's slowness, strength, and even the visual impression of the water patterns made as you wade through it. Similarly, when one of his cousins was teaching him how to boil eggs, she told him to put the eggs in the water 'when it starts to laugh'.

Gender Issues

Yerma is generally thought of as the second of a trilogy of Lorca's plays portraying the repression of women in Spanish rural life. In this play, as in *Blood Wedding* and *The House of Bernarda Alba,* Lorca portrays a world whose sexual mores trap women in an odiously repressive set of double standards that expect men to give full rein to their sexuality but savagely punish any woman who expresses hers. The central characters of these three plays, on the contrary, are all women whose sexuality is denied them, women trapped in a repressive society which denies them the possibility of life itself.

If we are to understand this fully, we must again try to put it into the context of Lorca's own life and experience. By all accounts he was, in some respects, a very solitary child. Long periods of ill health kept him in isolation from other children; and besides he suffered from a slight deformity. He had extremely flat feet, and one leg was slightly shorter than the other, which meant he walked with a very characteristic sway.

Like many a lonely child, he took refuge in the richness of his imagination; something all the more important to him as he grew older and attended secondary school where he was bullied and ridiculed by some of his more brutal classmates. They said he was effeminate and gave him the nickname of 'Federica'.

As he grew older, his inner isolation was deepened by the realisation of his homosexuality, and this led to a profound inner anguish which it is important we make the imaginative effort to understand.

The machismo of Spanish culture has been traditionally associated with a deep loathing of homosexuality which has only recently begun to dissipate. Even as recently as 1971, I remember a male friend in Granada telling me that, 'To be homosexual is the greatest misfortune that can befall a man.'

In the far more traditional Spain of the twenties and thirties, Lorca's sexuality was a source of profound shame, a secret he of necessity had to conceal from his parents and from everyone except his most intimate friends.

This meant that when he felt attracted to someone, he was not able to reach out and touch them; not able to express tenderness or affection; not able to put his arm round someone in the street; not able to kiss them. It meant every sexual encounter had to happen in secret and ran the risk of exposure and betrayal. In short, it meant being denied the most fundamental of human freedoms. And these are the very same freedoms denied to Yerma in this play. So in the play, Lorca is making a statement about the situation of women suffering repression; and it is also important we find the connections between their situation and that of the homosexual suffering repression in a homophobic society.

Yerma on Stage

The play opened in the Teatro Español in Madrid on 29 December 1934.

It was a highly charged political event. Both the dress rehearsal and the opening night were attended by many prominent literary and political figures of the left, together with hecklers from the right, who hurled homophobic insults at both Lorca and his leading actress, Margarita Xirgu. The great film director Luis Buñuel was also present, in agony from sciatica. The days of his association with Lorca were long over; true to form, he hated the play and walked, or rather limped, out at the end of the first scene of Act Two. The audience, and critics of the left, all adored it. The play was a huge commercial success and ran for more than 130 performances. The right-wing press, however, loathed it, and it became the focus of vicious attacks. It cemented Lorca's reputation among the right as a left-wing homosexual degenerate and in that sense contributed to the hatred that led to his assassination.

When it opened in Barcelona a few months later, it became the focus of Catalan nationalism. It is curious how so apparently apolitical a play should become the focus of such intense political passions – and continued to be so long after Lorca's death.

From 1939 onwards, the fascist dictatorship that governed Spain after the Civil War did everything it could to suppress Lorca's writing. Performance of his plays was not permitted for many years, though *Yerma* was the first play to break through the barrier of censorship. After immense difficulties, this performance took place in the Teatro Eslava in Madrid in autumn 1960. It was only allowed on condition there was no publicity, and the theatre was surrounded by armed police. Aurora Bautista, the actress in the leading role, still remained profoundly moved by the emotions of that first night in an interview she gave twenty-four years later, in 1984: 'It was so profoundly moving . . . the first performance of a work by Lorca since the end of the Civil

War . . . At the end, a basket of red flowers was left on the stage and everyone shouted: "Federico! Federico!"'

Another justly celebrated production was that directed by Victor García in 1971 and performed by Núria Espert. The production dispensed with the realistic settings specified in the text. Instead, it was all performed on something resembling a gigantic spider's web that could transform into all the settings the play demands, and which embodied the entrapment of the central character.

I was fortunate enough to see its revival in Edinburgh in 1986 on the night of the fiftieth anniversary of Federico's murder. It changed my artistic life for ever.

Looking back, I understand it was because it enabled me to see how it was possible to create theatre that is unashamedly emotional and absolutely not tied to being literally representational.

This is a kind of theatre that remains quite alien to the British tradition. Reading Michael Billington's *Guardian* review of the production of the play at the National Theatre the following year, with its 'tasteful gypsy dancing accompanied by a decorous trio on guitar and violin' makes one understand just how much the play is wonderfully un-English.

It is undeniably a real gift for the right female actor; probably the most successful English-speaking production has been Helena Kaut-Howson's staging at London's Arcola Theatre in 2006 with Kathryn Hunter in the title role.

It remains an extraordinarily demanding play to stage, and perhaps it is tempting to dismiss it as outdated.

But it is worth remembering that the majority of women in the contemporary world still live under conditions of patriarchy as oppressive as those Lorca describes; and so it remains, very defiantly, a fierce act of resistance. Lorca's profound compassion for humanity and his passionate protest on behalf of those suffering oppression of all kinds need to be heard more than ever.

Translator's Thanks

Thanks are due to Thomas Bailey, Thomas Wells and Alex Haigh, who insisted I finish this translation in time for their production in the Donald Roy Theatre, University of Hull, in February 2009. The following cast and production members also helped me to revise it: Busola Afolabi, Aimee Brehany, Ailsa Campbell, Kelly-Anne Chambers, Hannah Charter, Katie Driver, Emma Filby, Laura Fletcher, Sarah Gosnell, Jodie Howard, Joel Keating, Sam Kenny, Jess Pendlebury, Joel Redgrave, Rosie Tinker, Katie Waller, Kimberley Waller, Harriet Warnock, Sarah Williams and Hannah Wood.

Jo Clifford

Lorca: Key Dates

1898   5 June, Federico García Lorca born in Fuente Vaqueros, near Granada, Spain.

1909   His family move to Granada.

1914   Lorca enters Granada University to study law, on his father's insistence. Lorca had wanted to study music.

1919   Lorca enters the Residencia de Estudiantes in Madrid.

1920   22 March, Lorca's first play, *The Butterfly's Evil Spell*, opens in Madrid. It is a catastrophic failure.

1921   Publication of Lorca's first book of poems, *Libro de poemas.*

1922   The painter, Salvador Dalí, then eighteen, arrives in Madrid. He and Lorca become close friends.

1924–5   Lorca completes two more plays: *Mariana Pineda* and *The Shoemaker's Amazing Wife.*

1927   *Mariana Pineda* finally produced. It is an astonishing success.

1928   Publication of *Gypsy Ballads.*

1929   *The Love of Don Perlimplín* is about to be produced in Madrid, but the theatre is closed by the dictatorship.

Lorca leaves for New York, where he witnesses the Wall Street crash.

1930   Lorca returns to Spain via Cuba.

1931   Collapse of the dictatorship: establishment of the Spanish Republic.

1932   Lorca sets up La Barraca theatre company and begins touring the villages of Spain with productions of plays by Lope de Vega, Tirso de Molina and Calderón.

1933   Triumphant first production of *Blood Wedding*. Hitler's rise to power in Germany.

1933–4 Lorca visits Argentina, where his work is triumphantly received.

1934   The opening night of *Yerma* scandalises right-wing and traditional Catholic opinion.

1936   Successful opening of *Doña Rosita the Spinster*. Growing political unrest in Spain. Lorca writes *The House of Bernarda Alba*.

1936   14 July, Lorca returns to his parents in Granada.

        17 July, reads *The House of Bernarda Alba* to his friends in Granada.

        18 July, rebel right-wing uprising led by General Franco marks beginning of Civil War.

        23 July, right-wing rebels take over Granada.

        18 August, Federico García Lorca murdered by fascists.

For Further Reading

The experience of translating Lorca always leaves me profoundly aware of the deficiencies of any translation. Those wishing to make contact with the play in its original language should use this edition as their starting point: *Yerma*, edited by Robin Warner, Manchester University Press, 1994.

The best guide to Lorca's life is Ian Gibson's magnificent biography: *Federico García Lorca: A Life*, Faber, 1989.

His brother's memoir has been translated by Christopher Maurer: *In the Green Morning: Memories of Federico*, by Francisco García Lorca, Peter Owen, 1989.

A good academic introduction to Lorca's plays is Gwynne Edwards' *The Theatre Beneath the Sand*, Marion Boyars, 1989.

An excellent contemporary introduction to his work as a dramatist is Maria M. Delgado's *Federico García Lorca*, Routledge Modern and Contemporary Dramatists, London, 2008.

Gay themes in Lorca's work are explored in *Lorca and the Gay Imagination* by Paul Binding, GMP Books, 1985.

There are a great many available translations of Lorca's poetry. One of the best is *Poet in New York* (bilingual edition), translated by Greg Simon and Steven F. White, Viking, 1988.

An interesting collection of essays and creative responses, including discussions of the problems of translating Lorca is *Fire, Blood and the Alphabet: One Hundred Years of Lorca*, ed. Doggart and Thompson, Durham University Press, 2000.

YERMA

(Barren)

*A Tragic Poem in Three Acts
and Six Scenes*

To
Marni Robertson
another fierce woman of courage

J.C.

Characters

(in order of appearance)

YERMA
SHEPHERD
BOY CHILD
JUAN
MARIA
VICTOR
PAGAN OLD WOMAN
GIRL 1
GIRL 2
WASHERWOMAN 1
WASHERWOMAN 2
WASHERWOMAN 3
WASHERWOMAN 4
WASHERWOMAN 5
WASHERWOMAN 6
SISTER 1
SISTER 2
DOLORES
OLD WOMAN 1
OLD WOMAN 2
WOMAN 1
WOMAN 2
VILLAGE GIRLS
MALE MASK
FEMALE MASK
BOY
MAN 1
MAN 2

WOMEN, GIRLS, A CROWD

ACT ONE

Scene One

As the curtain rises, we see YERMA *asleep with a sewing basket at her feet.*

The stage is strangely lit, as if in a dream. A SHEPHERD *enters on tiptoe and stares at* YERMA. *He holds the hand of a* BOY CHILD *dressed in white. The clock strikes.*

As the SHEPHERD *leaves the stage, the blue light of the dream transforms into the happy daylight of a spring morning.* YERMA *wakes up.*

SONG (*from within*).
    Rock-a-bye baby
    Let's go and hide
    In a tiny wee housey
    Where we'll shelter inside.

YERMA. Juan. Can you hear me? Juan.

JUAN. Coming.

YERMA. It's time.

JUAN. Have they let out the goats?

YERMA. Yes.

JUAN. See you later. (*About to go.*)

YERMA. Won't you have some milk?

JUAN. Milk?

YERMA. You work so hard and it wears you out.

JUAN. Men have to work hard. That's how we get to be strong. Strong as iron.

YERMA. Yes. But not you. You weren't like this when we married. Now you're so pale. As if the sun never touched you. I wish you'd go down to the river and swim. Or climb onto the roof when the rain falls. Two years we've been married and every day you look worse. More dried up and withered. As if you were shrinking.

JUAN. Finished?

YERMA (*getting up*). Don't be offended. If I was ill I'd love you to look after me. I'd love you to say: 'My wife's ill. I'm going to kill a lamb to make her a nice meat stew.' Or: 'My wife's ill. I'm making up a tub of goose fat to rub on her chest. It'll help her feel better.' 'I'm going to take her a sheepskin to keep her feet warm.' That's how I am. And that's why I want to take care of you.

JUAN. And I thank you.

YERMA. But you won't let yourself be looked after.

JUAN. Why should I? There's nothing wrong with me. You just imagine things. I work hard. That's all there is to it. And each year I get a little older.

YERMA. Yes. Each year . . . and you and me, we carry on year after year . . .

JUAN (*smiling*). Of course we do. And we're doing well. The farm's really making money. And we don't have the expense of children.

YERMA. No. No, we don't have children . . . Juan!

JUAN. What?

YERMA. Is it because I don't love you?

JUAN. No. I know you love me.

YERMA. I know girls who were shaking all over before
they went to bed with their husbands and who cried
and cried. And did I cry before I went before I went to
bed with you? No I did not. And when I slipped in
between our fine linen sheets I sang for joy. And didn't
I say: 'The bedclothes smell fresh as apples?'

JUAN. That's what you said!

YERMA. I wasn't sorry to leave my mother and that
made her cry. It was true. No one was happier than
me to get married. But still . . .

JUAN. Don't say it. I've got enough on my hands without
having to listen to them saying . . .

YERMA. Don't tell me what they're saying. And I know
it's not true. The rain falls on the stones, it falls and it
falls, and they become soft earth and a place where the
gillyflower grow. And people say they're no use to
anybody but I can see their yellow flowers dancing in
the sunshine.

JUAN. We have to be patient.

YERMA. Yes. Patient. And loving too!

YERMA *embraces her husband and kisses him. She takes the
lead.*

JUAN. If you need anything just tell me. I'll bring it you.
You know I don't like you going out.

YERMA. I never go out.

JUAN. You're better off at home.

YERMA. I know.

JUAN. The street is for people with nothing better to do.

YERMA (*sombrely*). Obviously.

The husband leaves. YERMA *goes to her sewing basket. She passes her hand over her belly, lets out a lovely yawn as she lifts her arms to the sky. And sits down to sew.*

Where are you, my baby, my dear one?
On the slope of the cold cold hill
What are you needing my baby, my dear one?
To cuddle your dress with its frill.

She threads her needle.

The tree waves its branches in the sun
The fountain's clear water does run, does run.

As if she was talking to a child:

The dog barks in the doorway
The wind sings in the trees
The sheep baa to their shepherd
My hair waves up to the moon.
What do you want, my baby forlorn?

Pause.

'I want the white mountains, I want your white breasts'
The tree waves its branches in the sun
The fountain's clear water does run, does run.

Sewing

I'll say yes to you, my baby, my loved one
Though for you I've been battered and broken
Here in my womb it hurts me, my dear one

My baby, where your first cradle will be.
When will you come, my loved one, come to me, come
    to me?

Pause.

'When your skin smells of the white jasmine tree'
The tree waves its branches in the sun
The fountain's clear water does run, does run.

YERMA *keeps singing.* MARIA *enters through the door,
carrying a parcel of clothes.*

YERMA. Where have you been?

MARIA. The shop.

YERMA. So early?

MARIA. I wanted to camp out on the street till opening
    time! Guess what I've been buying!

YERMA. Coffee, butter, sugar, bread . . .

MARIA. No. Not that. I've been buying material,
    ribbons, bits of lace, coloured wool to make those
    fancy bobbles . . . My husband had the money and
    gave it me himself.

YERMA. You're going to make a blouse.

MARIA. No. Can't you guess?

YERMA. No.

MARIA. It's because . . . He's coming . . . (*She's silent a
    moment, and hides her face.*)

    YERMA *gets up and looks at her admiringly.*

YERMA. After only five months!

MARIA. Yes.

YERMA. And you knew?

MARIA. Of course I did.

YERMA. And how did you know? What did it feel like?

MARIA. I don't know. (*Pause.*) It felt bad.

YERMA. It felt bad. (*Clinging onto her.*) But . . . when did
he come? Tell me . . . Maybe you were thinking of
something else . . .

MARIA. Yes. Thinking of something else . . .

YERMA. You were singing, maybe? I'm always singing.
What about you? Tell me.

MARIA. Don't ask me. Have you ever held a little bird
cupped in your hand?

YERMA. Yes.

MARIA. Well, it's like that . . . only it's inside. In your
blood.

YERMA. How beautiful! (*She looks at her in wonder.*)

MARIA. I don't know.

YERMA. Don't know what?

MARIA. Don't know what to do. I'll ask my mother.

YERMA. Why ask her? She's old and she'll have
forgotten all about it. Don't overdo things and when
you breathe, breathe really gently as if in your mouth
you were holding a rose.

MARIA. You know something? They say that when he
gets a bit bigger he'll start giving me little pushes with
his feet.

YERMA. And that's when you love him more than ever.
That's when you say: he's my son!

MARIA. And on top of everything I feel really
embarrassed.

YERMA. What does your husband say?

MARIA. Nothing.

YERMA. Does he love you?

MARIA. He never says so, but when he comes close to
me his eyes kind of shiver like two green leaves.

YERMA. And did he know that you . . . ?

MARIA. Yes.

YERMA. How did he know?

MARIA. I don't know. But that first night we were
married he kept telling me, with his mouth next to my
cheek, so it seems to me that my son is a dove of light
that he poured into my ear.

YERMA. You're so lucky!

MARIA. But you know more about this than I do.

YERMA. And what's the use of it?

MARIA. It's a shame! And why should that be? Of all
the girls who got married when you did you're the
only one . . .

YERMA. That's just how it is. Obviously there's still
time. It took Elena three years, and then there were
other girls in my mother's day who took much longer,
but to have to wait two years and twenty days like me
is just too long. It's not right. I shouldn't have to burn

myself up like this. Often I go out the door barefoot just so I can tread the earth. I don't know why. If this goes on like this, I'm going to make myself ill.

MARIA. Oh, come here, love! You're talking like you were old. And you're not! There's no point worrying about these things. One of my mum's sisters had her first when she was forty, and you should have seen what a lovely boy!

YERMA (*with anxious longing*). What was he like?

MARIA. He used to yell like a little bull, so loud he deafened us. And then he peed on us. And he pulled our hair, and when he was four months old he covered our faces with scratches.

YERMA (*laughing*). Things like that don't hurt.

MARIA. Well . . .

YERMA. No they don't! I once saw my sister breast-feeding her baby and her breast was all cracked and sore and it really hurt her. But it was good pain. It was full of life. She needed it to get better.

MARIA. They do say that your children make you suffer.

YERMA. That's not true. It's only weak and whiny mothers say things like that. Why do they have children anyway? Having a son is not like having a bunch of flowers. We have to suffer to see them grow. I think they drink up half our blood. But that's good, healthy, beautiful. Every woman's got enough blood for four or five sons. And when they don't have them this blood turns bad. Like mine.

MARIA. I don't know what's wrong with me.

YERMA. I've heard that first-time mothers get easily scared.

MARIA (*shyly*). Maybe . . . But listen, I was wondering, since you're so good at sewing . . .

YERMA (*taking the bundle*). Fine. I'll cut out his baby clothes. What's in this?

MARIA. That's for his nappies.

YERMA. Good. (*She sits down.*)

MARIA. Thank you. See you soon.

She goes up to YERMA, *who lovingly places her hands on her belly.*

YERMA. Be careful on the cobblestones in the street.

MARIA. Goodbye. (*She kisses her, and goes out.*)

YERMA. Come back soon!

YERMA is in the same position as she was at the beginning. She picks up her scissors and starts to cut the material. Enter VICTOR.

Good morning, Victor.

VICTOR (*a man of depth and gravity*). Where's Juan?

YERMA. In the fields.

VICTOR. What are you sewing?

YERMA. Some nappies.

VICTOR (*smiling*). Fancy that.

YERMA (*laughing*). I'm going to edge them with lacework.

VICTOR. If it's a girl you'll give her your name.

YERMA (*trembling*). What?

VICTOR. I'm happy for you.

YERMA (*as if suffocating with her feeling*). No . . . no, they're not for me. They're for Maria's son.

VICTOR. Well, maybe she'll set you a good example! This house needs a child.

YERMA (*with anguish*). Yes. That is what this house needs.

VICTOR. So. Keep trying. Tell your husband not to be so concerned with work. He wants to get money and he'll get it all right, but who will he leave it to? I'm taking my sheep out to pasture. Tell Juan to pick up the two he bought from me. And as for the other thing . . . Tell him to dig deep! (*He goes out smiling.*)

YERMA (*with passion*). Exactly! Tell him to dig deep!

YERMA *gets up thoughtfully and goes to the spot where* VICTOR *has been. She breathes in deep, as if breathing in fresh air from the mountain. Then she goes to the other side of the room, as if she's looking for something, and from there she goes back to her seat and picks up her sewing. She starts to sew with her eyes fixed on the same point.*

I'll say yes to you, my baby, my loved one
Though for you I've been battered and broken
Here in my womb it hurts me, my dear one
My baby, where your first cradle will be.
When will you come, my loved one, come to me, come to me?
'When your skin smells of the white jasmine tree.'

Curtain.

Scene Two

In the fields. Enter YERMA. *She carries a basket.*

Enter the PAGAN OLD WOMAN.

YERMA. Good morning.

OLD WOMAN. Good morning, my lovely. Where are
    you off to?

YERMA. I've just taken my husband his midday meal . . .
    He's working in the field.

OLD WOMAN. You been married long?

YERMA. Three years.

OLD WOMAN. Got any children?

YERMA. No.

OLD WOMAN. Oh well. You will.

YERMA (*with deep anxiety*). You really think so?

OLD WOMAN. Why ever not? (*She sits down.*) I've just
    taken my husband his dinner too. He's old. Still
    working. I've got nine sons like sunbeams. But because
    they're all male, here's me still working like a donkey.

YERMA. You live the other side of the river.

OLD WOMAN. That's me. By the water mill. Who's
    your family?

YERMA. I'm Enrique the shepherd's daughter.

OLD WOMAN. Ah. Enrique the shepherd. I knew him.
    Good people. The kind that get up, work hard, eat
    their daily bread and die. No days off, no days out,

nothing. Fiestas are for other people. Never them. Silent creatures. I could have married one of your uncles. But no. He wasn't for me. My skirts swing in the wind. My mouth loves a melon. My belly loves a pastry. My feet love dancing. See me, so often I've been at my front door just as soon as the day is dawning, ready to dance to the tambourine. The tambourine I could swear I heard playing, coming closer. Closer and closer. But then it's turned out to be just the wind. (*She laughs.*) You'll think me strange. I've had two husbands and fourteen sons. Six of them died. But I'm not sad. I'd like to live for ever. What I say is: look at the trees. How long they last. Look at a house of stone. How long it lasts. And then look at us, poor bloody women falling to bits for no reason at all.

YERMA. I'd like to ask you something.

OLD WOMAN. Would you? (*She looks at her.*) I know what you're going to say. These are things no one can talk about. (*She gets up.*)

YERMA (*stopping her*). Why not? Listening to you makes me trust you. For a long time now I've wanted to have a proper talk with an old woman like you. Because I want to find out. I really do. And you can tell me . . .

OLD WOMAN. What?

YERMA (*lowering her voice*). What you know. Why am I barren? Is there nothing else I can do with my life but look after budgies or put beautifully ironed curtains up in my window? No. You have to tell me what I need to do, because I will do whatever I have to. Even if you ask me to hit nails into the whites of my eyes.

OLD WOMAN. Me? I don't know nothing. I just opened
my legs and started singing. Children come like the
rain. Oooh . . . look at your body. Your beautiful body.
Is there anyone so blind as to say otherwise? Step
outside, and a stallion will neigh at the end of the
street. Uy! Leave me alone, girl, don't make me speak.
I am thinking things I do not wish to say out loud.

YERMA. Why not? With my husband, that's all I talk
about.

OLD WOMAN. Listen. You like your husband?

YERMA. What do you mean?

OLD WOMAN. Do you like him? Do you want to be
with him? Do you desire him?

YERMA. I don't know.

OLD WOMAN. When he comes to you does he make
you shiver? When his mouth comes to yours do you go
all dreamy? Tell me.

YERMA. No. I never felt like that. Never.

OLD WOMAN. Never? Not even when you were
dancing?

YERMA (*trying to remember*). Maybe . . . once . . . with
Victor . . .

OLD WOMAN. Go on.

YERMA. He put his arm round my waist and I couldn't
say anything because I couldn't speak. And another
time, Victor again, when I was fourteen and he was
grown up, he picked me up to cross a stream and I
was shaking so much my teeth started chattering. But
the trouble was I felt ashamed.

OLD WOMAN. And your husband?

YERMA. With my husband it's something else again. My father gave me to him and I was happy. That's absolutely true. And the very first day I knew I was to be married to him I thought . . . I thought about children . . . And I looked at myself reflected in his eyes. Yes, and there I was, very small, at his bidding, as if I was my own child.

OLD WOMAN. Just the opposite to me. Perhaps that's why you haven't given birth. Listen, girl, when it comes to men you need to want them. They have to undo our hair and make us drink their mouths' saliva. That's what makes the world go round.

YERMA. Yours maybe, but not mine. I think things, many things, and I am sure the things I think my son will make come true. I gave myself to my husband for his sake, and I keep on giving myself just in case he comes. But never just to have pleasure.

OLD WOMAN. And that's why you're still empty!

YERMA. No. No, I'm not empty. I'm slowly filling with hate. Tell me, please, is it all my fault? Have I just got to keep looking for the man in the man? Is that all I can do? Or else, what are you supposed to think when he rolls over onto his side and goes to sleep, and you're just left there looking sadly up at the ceiling? Am I just supposed to keep on thinking of him, or of what could come out of my belly, shining? I don't know any more. Tell me. Please tell me. (*She kneels.*)

OLD WOMAN. Oh, you open flower! How lovely a creature you are! Let me be. Don't make me say more.

I don't want to talk to you any more. These are things to do with honour, and I won't harm anyone's honour. You'll know what to do. But whatever you do, you should try to be less innocent.

YERMA (*sad*). Girls like me, girls who grow up in the country . . . all the doors are shut and bolted shut in our face. It's all words left only half-spoken, gestures only half-made, because these are all things that you're just not supposed to know . . . And you too, you keep quiet too, and then off you go looking like you know, like you know the answer to everything, but won't say it, won't tell me, even though you know I am dying of thirst.

OLD WOMAN. I would talk to a woman who was calmer. But not to you. I'm an old woman and I know what I'm saying.

YERMA. Then God help me.

OLD WOMAN. God's no use to you, dear. I've no time for him. When are you going to understand he doesn't exist? He's no use to you. Only men are.

YERMA. But why are you saying this? Why?

OLD WOMAN (*going*). Although there should be a god, even if only a tiny one, so he could send down his lightning to burn up the men whose seed is rotten and who poison the joy of the fields.

YERMA. I don't know what you're trying to tell me.

OLD WOMAN. Never mind. I know. Don't be sad. Keep hoping. You're still very young. What am I supposed to do for you?

She goes.

Two GIRLS *appear.*

GIRL 1. We just keep bumping into people everywhere!

YERMA. It's the olive harvest, so the men are out in the fields. It's just the old people left inside.

GIRL 2. You going back to the village?

YERMA. Yes, that's where I'm going.

GIRL 1. I'm in a real hurry. I left my baby asleep in the house alone.

YERMA. Then run. You can't leave a baby on his own. What if he got eaten by a sow?

GIRL 1. We don't keep pigs. But you're right. I'll run home.

YERMA. Yes. Run. These things happen. You've surely left him locked in.

GIRL 1. Obviously.

YERMA. I don't think you know how fragile a little child is. Something that seems completely harmless to us can finish him off. The slightest thing: a little needle, a sip of water.

GIRL 1. Yes, you're right. I'm running. The thing is I don't always think things through.

YERMA. Go!

GIRL 2. You wouldn't talk like that if you had four or five.

YERMA. Why not? I'm sure I would. Even if I had forty.

GIRL 2. Anyway, you and me, without children, we're much better off.

YERMA. Not me.

GIRL 2. I am. What a lot of work they are! But then my mum keeps on making me drink these disgusting herbs to help me get pregnant, and in October we've got to go to the shrine of the saint they say gives children to those who sincerely ask for them. My mum'll ask. I won't.

YERMA. Why did you get married?

GIRL 2. Because they made me. They make all of us. If things go on like this, everyone'll be married except girls of five! That's how it is. But then anyway you really get married long before you go to the church. It's the old women. They just can't leave these things alone. I'm nineteen years old and I hate cooking and washing. But that's what I've got to do all day. Things I hate doing. And why? Why does my husband need to be my husband? We do exactly the same things we used to do before we got married. It's just old people's silliness.

YERMA. Shush. Don't say such things.

GIRL 2. You're going to say I'm mad too. 'Mad. She's mad!' (*Laughs.*) I'll tell you the only thing I've learned from life: that the whole world is stuck in their houses doing things they hate doing. People are so much better off out in the street. I go to the stream. I climb the tower to ring the bells, I can have a wee drink of anís.

YERMA. You're just a girl.

GIRL 2. Yes. Obviously, but I'm not mad. (*Laughs.*)

YERMA. Is it your mother who lives right up at the top of the village?

GIRL 2. Yes.

YERMA. In the very last house?

GIRL 2. Yes.

YERMA. What's her name?

GIRL 2. Dolores. Why do you want to know?

YERMA. I don't know. I was just . . .

GIRL 2. Look at you . . . Anyway, I'm off to give my husband his food. (*Laughs.*) It just goes to show. What a shame I can't just call him my man! Right? 'There she goes. Mad she is. Mad!' (*She goes off laughing cheerfully.*) Byee!

VICTOR'S VOICE (*singing*).
Shepherd, why sleep alone?
Shepherd, why sleep alone?
You'd sleep so much better
On my mattress at home.
Shepherd, why sleep alone?

YERMA (*listening*).
Shepherd, why sleep alone?
Shepherd, why sleep alone?
You'd sleep so much better
On my mattress at home.
Your shirt is stiff with frost,
Shepherd, and your mattress of grey stone.
Winter's splintered straw for a blanket

For your pillow, just thistles and thorns.
You spend the winter's night alone.
If you hear a woman sighing
See a woman in your dreams
It's just the wind blowing
The water eddying in the streams.

About to leave, she bumps into VICTOR *as he enters.*

VICTOR. Where's she going, this beauty?

YERMA. Was it you who was singing?

VICTOR. It was me.

YERMA. You sing so well! It's the first time I've heard you.

VICTOR. Is it?

YERMA. Such a strong voice. It's like a mountain stream. It just flows out your mouth so naturally.

VICTOR. I'm happy.

YERMA. It's true.

VICTOR. And you are sad.

YERMA. No, I'm not sad. But I do have reason to be.

VICTOR. A husband who's even sadder than you are.

YERMA. Him, yes. He's a dried-up kind of person.

VICTOR. He's always been like that. (*Pause.* YERMA *has sat down.*) Did you come to bring him his meal?

YERMA. Yes. (*She looks at him. Pause.*) What happened there? (*She points to his face.*)

VICTOR. Where?

YERMA (*getting up and going to* VICTOR). Here . . . on your cheek. It looks like a burn.

VICTOR. It's nothing.

YERMA. I just wondered.

Pause.

VICTOR. Maybe I caught the sun . . .

YERMA. Maybe . . .

Pause. The silence deepens and without the slightest outward sign an intense struggle begins between the two of them.

(*Trembling.*) Do you hear?

VICTOR. Hear what?

YERMA. There's a baby crying.

VICTOR (*listening*). I can't hear it.

YERMA. I could have sworn I heard a baby cry.

VICTOR. Did you?

YERMA. Very close. As if it was drowning.

VICTOR. There's always a lot of kids round here. They come to rob the fruit trees.

YERMA. It wasn't them. It was a baby.

Pause.

VICTOR. I can't hear anything.

YERMA. I must be hearing things.

She stares at him, and VICTOR *looks at her, and then slowly looks away, as if afraid.*

Enter JUAN.

JUAN. What are you doing here?

YERMA. Talking.

VICTOR. Good day. (*He goes.*)

JUAN. You should be at home.

YERMA. It was nice here.

JUAN. I can't imagine what was so nice.

YERMA. I was listening to the birds singing.

JUAN. People are going to start to talk.

YERMA (*fiercely*). Juan, what are you implying?

JUAN. I'm not talking about you. I'm talking about what people might say.

YERMA. I hope they all choke!

JUAN. Don't use such expressions. A woman shouldn't speak like that. They make you ugly.

YERMA. I wish I was a woman!

JUAN. We won't talk about it further. Go back home.

Pause.

YERMA. As you wish. When shall I expect you?

JUAN. I won't come home tonight. I've to be out here to water the crops. There's not much water, and tonight it's my turn to get it. I need to stay here till dawn to make sure no one steals it. I'll be here till dawn. Go to bed and sleep.

YERMA (*with deep feeling*). I'll sleep! (*She goes.*)

Curtain.

ACT TWO

Scene One

A rushing stream in which the village women do their washing. The WASHERWOMEN *are on various levels. They sing with the curtain still closed.*

WASHERWOMEN.
Cold is the water
Washing this hour
Warm is your laughter
Like jasmine flower.

WASHERWOMAN 1. I don't like to gossip . . .

WASHERWOMAN 3. But everyone's doing it.

WASHERWOMAN 4. And there's no harm in it.

WASHERWOMAN 5. No smoke without fire.

WASHERWOMAN 4. No fire without smoke.

They laugh.

WASHERWOMAN 5. So people say.

WASHERWOMAN 1. But no one really knows.

WASHERWOMAN 4. One thing for sure is that the husband has brought in his two sisters to live with them.

WASHERWOMAN 5. The old maids?

WASHERWOMAN 4. Them. The ones who look after the church and now have to look after his wife. I wouldn't want them in my house.

WASHERWOMAN 1. Why not?

WASHERWOMAN 4. They're so creepy. They're like those slimy plants with the big green leaves that you see growing on a freshly dug grave. They're greasy with candle wax. I think they must cook with the oil from the lamps in church.

WASHERWOMAN 3. And they're in her house already?

WASHERWOMAN 4. Since yesterday. And the husband's out working on his land.

WASHERWOMAN 1. Can someone tell me what's supposed to have happened?

WASHERWOMAN 5. Remember how cold it was the night before last? Well, she spent the whole night out in it. Sitting on her own doorstep. She spent the night before last sitting out on the doorstep in spite of the cold.

WASHERWOMAN 1. But why?

WASHERWOMAN 4. Because she can't stand being inside her own house.

WASHERWOMAN 5. She's just a withered old bitch that'll never have kids. They're all the same. She should stay out of sight and mind her own business. But instead they go walking naked on their rooftops or sit out all night on their doorsteps.

WASHERWOMAN 1. What right have you to say things like that? It's not her fault she doesn't have children.

WASHERWOMAN 4. People have children who really want them. There's just some that are too weak, too delicate, too soft and too posh to be able to bear having a stretch mark.

They laugh.

WASHERWOMAN 3. So they put on red lipstick and black eye-shadow and their best low-cut dress and go off looking for another man who is not their husband.

WASHERWOMAN 5. And that's the way it is.

WASHERWOMAN 1. But have any of you actually seen her with another man?

WASHERWOMAN 4. Well, we haven't. But people have.

WASHERWOMAN 1. Strange how it's always someone else!

WASHERWOMAN 5. It's twice she's been seen with a man. That's what they say.

WASHERWOMAN 2. And what were they doing?

WASHERWOMAN 4. Talking.

WASHERWOMAN 1. Talking is not a crime.

WASHERWOMAN 5. But they were also looking. And looking is something else. My mother used to tell me. A woman looking at a bunch of flowers is one thing. A woman looking at a man's thighs is quite another. And she looks at him.

WASHERWOMAN 1. But who?

WASHERWOMAN 4. Someone. Don't you know?

Think about it. Do you want me to spell it out?
(*Laughter.*) And even when she's not looking at him,
because she's on her own, and he's not in front of her,
he's still pictured in her eyes.

WASHERWOMAN 1. You're a liar!

A moment of fierce conflict.

WASHERWOMAN 5. What about the husband?

WASHERWOMAN 3. It's like he was deaf and blind.
Paralysed. Like a lizard in the noonday sun.

They laugh.

WASHERWOMAN 1. If only they had children. All this
would sort itself out.

WASHERWOMAN 2. All this would sort itself out if
some people knew their place.

WASHERWOMAN 4. It gets worse and worse in that
house. Hour by hour. It's like being in hell. Her and
her two sisters-in-law never say a word to each other.
They spend all day whitewashing the walls, polishing
the coppers, cleaning all the glasses and waxing the
floors. And the more the house gleams on the outside,
the muckier it is on the inside.

WASHERWOMAN 1. It's his fault. It's his. When a
husband can't father a child he needs to take care of
his wife.

WASHERWOMAN 4. No. It's her fault. She's got a
tongue like a razor.

WASHERWOMAN 1. What's got into you to make you
say such horrible things?

WASHERWOMAN 4. And what's got into you to make you think you can tell me what to do?

WASHERWOMAN 5. Quiet!

Laughter.

WASHERWOMAN 1. If I had a darning needle I'd sew up the mouths of malicious tongues.

WASHERWOMAN 5. Shut up!

WASHERWOMAN 4. And I'd cover the breasts of hypocrites.

WASHERWOMAN 5. Be quiet! Can't you see who's coming? It's the aunts!

Mutterings. YERMA's *two* SISTERS-IN-LAW *enter. They are dressed in mourning. They begin to wash in the midst of the silence. We hear goat bells.*

WASHERWOMAN 1. Have the shepherds gone?

WASHERWOMAN 3. Yes. The flocks are all leaving now.

WASHERWOMAN 4 (*breathing in*). I love the smell of sheep.

WASHERWOMAN 3. Do you?

WASHERWOMAN 4. And why not? It smells of such familiar things. Just as I like the smell of the red mud brought down by the river in winter.

WASHERWOMAN 3. You're crazy.

WASHERWOMAN 5 (*looking out*). They've joined all the flocks together.

WASHERWOMAN 4. As if to flood everywhere with wool. They trample over everything. If the young wheat had eyes, it would tremble to see them coming.

WASHERWOMAN 3. And how they run! What a crowd!

WASHERWOMAN 1. Out they all go. None are left behind.

WASHERWOMAN 4. Wait . . . I'm not sure . . . Yes. there's one flock missing.

WASHERWOMAN 5. Whose?

WASHERWOMAN 4. Victor's.

The two SISTERS-IN-LAW *raise their heads to see.*

Cold is the water
Washing this hour
Warm is your laughter
Like jasmine flower.

I'm dreaming of living
In the tiny white snowfall
Of the jasmine's white flower.

WASHERWOMAN 1.
Pity the woman whose breasts are dry
Barren as the desert
Under the empty sky

WASHERWOMAN 5.
Tell me does your husband
Keep seed in your house
So the water starts singing
In your linen blouse

WASHERWOMAN 6.
Your blouse floats like a ship
By the bend of the river
Its sails fill with wind

WASHERWOMAN 3.
The clothes of my baby
I've come here to wash
They're teaching the water
To be clear as glass

WASHERWOMAN 2.
My husband is coming
Down the high road to eat
A rose he will bring me
And I'll give him three

WASHERWOMAN 5.
My husband is coming
Down the low road to dine
His hands full of fire
Like hot coals are mine

WASHERWOMAN 4.
My husband is coming
Through the air to his bed
I give him red poppies
His roses are red

WASHERWOMAN 3.
Flower lies with flower
The summer heat warms the seed

WASHERWOMAN 4.
When winter sets the whole world shivering and shaking
Still the belly lies open to the birds that are waking

WASHERWOMAN 1.
  Time to be moaning in between the sheets

WASHERWOMAN 4.
  Time to be singing in the bed off the streets

WASHERWOMAN 5.
  When the man brings in bread and brings in the crown

WASHERWOMAN 4.
  When arms are embracing what's up and what's down

WASHERWOMAN 5.
  Because our throat is open to the golden light

WASHERWOMAN 4.
  The branches are bending, the flowers are bright

WASHERWOMAN 5.
  The mountains are covered by the wings of the wind.

WASHERWOMAN 6 (*appearing high up at the top of the torrent*).
  So a baby can melt
  The cold fingers of dawn

WASHERWOMAN 4.
  So the coral's branches of red
  Can crown our fierce heads

WASHERWOMAN 5.
  And the sailors sing gladness
  On the waves of the sea

WASHERWOMAN 1.
  A child, a little one

WASHERWOMAN 2.
  And the doves spread their wings

WASHERWOMAN 3.
A child laughing, a loved one

WASHERWOMAN 4.
And the men moving forward
Like bold rutting stags

WASHERWOMAN 5.
Oh, the joy the joy the joy
Of the round fertile belly!

WASHERWOMAN 2.
Oh, the joy the joy the joy
Of the navel, the tender cup of marvels!

WASHERWOMAN 1.
Pity the woman whose breasts are dry
Barren as the desert
Under the empty sky

WASHERWOMAN 4.
Let the child shine!

WASHERWOMAN 5.
Let him run!

WASHERWOMAN 4.
Let him shine again!

WASHERWOMAN 3.
Let him sing!

WASHERWOMAN 2.
Let him hide!

WASHERWOMAN 3.
Let him sing again.

WASHERWOMAN 6.
  Of the dawn that my baby
  Carries in his eyes!

WASHERWOMAN 4 (*and they all sing with her in chorus*).
  Cold is the water
  Washing this hour
  Warm is your laughter
  Like jasmine flower.

They all laugh together and beat the clothes together to wash them on the stones.

Curtain.

Scene Two

YERMA's *house. Nightfall.* JUAN *is sitting. His two* SISTERS *stand.*

JUAN. You're saying she just went out?

  SISTER 1 *nods in reply.*

  She must be getting water from the well. But you know I don't like her to go out alone. (*Pause.*) You can lay the table.

  SISTER 2 *goes out.*

  I've worked hard for the food on my table. (*To* SISTER 1.) Yesterday was a hard day. I was pruning the apple trees. At the end of the day I started to wonder why I work so hard when I can't pick an apple and eat it myself. I've had enough. (*He passes his hands over his face. Pause.*) Still not back . . . One of you should go out with her, because that's why you're here. That's why you're eating at my table and drinking my wine. My life is out in the fields but my honour and self-respect are here. And my honour is also your honour.

SISTER 1 *nods her head.*

Don't take it to heart.

YERMA *comes in with two large water jugs. She stops on the threshold.*

Have you come from the spring?

YERMA. So we could have some cool water with our meal.

Enter SISTER 2.

How is the land?

JUAN. Yesterday I was pruning the apple trees.

YERMA *puts down the water jugs. Pause.*

YERMA. Are you staying in?

JUAN. I have to take care of the flock. You know that's the owner's responsibility.

YERMA. I know that only too well. There's no need to say it again.

JUAN. Each man must live his life.

YERMA. And each woman must live hers. I'm not asking you to stay at home. I have all I need here. Your sisters feed me very well. Roast lamb, soft white bread and the finest cheese on the menu for your wife, and good green grass on the hillside for your sheep. You can set your mind at rest.

JUAN. Having your mind at rest means living in peace.

YERMA. And don't you?

JUAN. No.

YERMA. There's no point talking about it.

JUAN. But don't you know how I want life to be? Sheep in the sheepfold. Women in the home. You go out too much. Haven't I said that again and again?

YERMA. Yes. So you have. Women in the home. When their homes are not like a grave. When beds get broken and sheets get worn out with use. But not here. Every night when I go to bed, my bed is as new and as unused as if we had just bought it in a shop in the city.

JUAN. You know very well I'm right to complain. That I'm right to stay on my guard!

YERMA. On your guard against what? I don't do you any harm. I live under your thumb, and what I suffer I keep to myself. Nailed to my flesh. Every day that passes will be worse. And we'll never talk about it. I'll do what I can to bear what I have to bear, but don't ask me for any more. If all of a sudden I could turn into an old woman with a withered mouth, I might be able to smile and live with you. But just now, just leave me alone. Leave me with what's nailed into me.

JUAN. You are talking in a way I cannot understand. I don't deprive you of anything. I'm always asking the neighbours for things I know you like to have. I'm not perfect, I know that, but I want to live with you peacefully and quietly. Without fuss. I want to sleep in the open and know that you are sleeping too.

YERMA. I don't sleep. I can't sleep.

JUAN. Is there anything you need? Tell me. (*Pause.*)
Answer!

YERMA (*with a clear intention and looking fixedly at her
husband*). Yes. Yes, there is something.

Pause.

JUAN. It's always that. After more than five years. I'd
almost forgotten all about it.

YERMA. But you are not me. The men have another
life: with their sheep and their crops. The things they
talk about. But with us women there's just children.
And how to look after them. That's all there is.

JUAN. Not everyone's the same. Why don't you look after
one of your brother's children? I wouldn't mind.

YERMA. I don't want to look after other people's
children. I can feel my arms freezing when I hold them.

JUAN. And that's exactly the attitude that's distressing
you. So you end up not behaving as you ought. And
instead you keep banging your head against a stone
wall.

YERMA. A stone wall which shouldn't be a wall. The
fact it's there is a kind of crime. When what it should
be is a basket of flowers and a jug of sweet water.

JUAN. All I ever get from you is anguish and anxiety and
grief. But at the end of the day you have just got to get
used to things.

YERMA. I came here not to get used to things. When
they tie a scarf round my head to stop my mouth

dropping open. When they have to jam my hands together inside my coffin. That's when I'll have got used to things.

JUAN. So what do you want?

YERMA. I want to drink water, and there is no water to drink and no glass to drink it in. I want to climb to the summit of the mountain, and I have no feet to walk with. I want to embroider my dress, and I have neither needle nor thread.

JUAN. You're just not a proper woman and you'll ruin any man who can't stand up to you.

YERMA. I don't know who I am. Let me be. Let me try to unburden myself. I have failed you in nothing.

JUAN. I don't want people to point the finger at me. That is why I want this door to be kept shut and for everyone to stay in their home.

SISTER 1 *slowly comes onto the stage and goes up to a glass-fronted cupboard.*

YERMA. Talking to people is not a crime.

JUAN. But it can look like one.

SISTER 2 *enters, goes to the water container, and fills up a jug.*

(*Lowering his voice.*) I haven't the strength for this. When they talk to you, keep your mouth shut. Remember you're a married woman.

YERMA (*astounded*). Me? Married?

JUAN. And remember: families need honour and they need self-respect, and these things are everyone's responsibility.

SISTER 2 *slowly leaves with the water jug.*

But in the very veins of our body our honour flows
sluggish and weak.

SISTER 1 *leaves with a serving dish, in a way that almost
recalls a church procession. Pause.*

Forgive me.

YERMA *looks at her husband. He raises his head to look at
her. His gaze falters.*

Although you look at me in a way that means I should
not say 'Forgive me'. I should impose myself instead,
and lock you away. Because that's what being a
husband means.

The two SISTERS *appear in the doorway.*

YERMA. Please don't talk about it any more. Let's leave
these things be.

Pause.

JUAN. Let's go in to eat.

The two SISTERS *go inside. Pause.*

Did you hear me?

YERMA (*gently*). You eat with your sisters. I don't feel
hungry just now.

JUAN. Whatever you say. (*He goes in.*)

YERMA (*dreamily*).
   Oh, the road I travel is paved with thorn
   The door of love is shut against me
   I'm asking to suffer the birth pangs of a baby
   And all I'm given are limp flowers

Wilting under a half-formed moon!
These should be two springs of warm milk
But instead in my thickened coarsened flesh
They feel like the hoof beats of a wounded animal.
My breasts have been blinded.
They're doves without eyes or whiteness.
My blood is a prisoner going round and round my body
And my pulse nails thorns to my throat.
You have to come, my child, my loved one,
You have to come, like the ocean gives salt,
Trees give their fruit, and our wombs
Keep tender children safe in warm darkness
Like the cloud that carries sweet rain.

She looks towards the door.

Maria! Why are you rushing so fast by my door?

Enter MARIA.

MARIA. I'm carrying my baby and I can't bear to see you cry.

YERMA. I understand. (*She takes the baby and sits down.*)

MARIA. I'm so sorry I make you so envious.

YERMA. I'm not envious. I'm just poor.

MARIA. Don't cry.

YERMA. What else can I do when I see you and all the other women so full of flowers and me so useless in the midst of so much beauty!

MARIA. But you've other things in your life. If you'd just listen to me, you could be happy.

YERMA. The country woman who has no children is as

useless as a handful of thistles. And worse. There's a
kind of badness to her. And I'm saying that even
though I belong to this godforsaken wasteland.

MARIA *makes a move to take back her baby.*

Yes. Take him. He'll be happier with you. I don't seem
to have a mother's hands.

MARIA. Why are you telling me this?

YERMA (*getting up*). Because I'm weary, so weary of
having arms that are made to hold someone and that
I'm never able to use as they should. Because I just
can't bear it. It insults me, it humiliates and it degrades
me to see how the wheat comes to harvest and the
springs keep giving water and the sheep keep giving
birth to lambs and even the dogs. And it's like the
whole of the countryside is going out of its way to
show me its adorable sleepy warm babies, while
instead of the feeding mouth of my child here, and
here, all I feel is like the dull thud of a heavy hammer.

MARIA. I don't like what you're saying.

YERMA. You women who have children can't imagine
what it's like to be us who don't. You're just so
innocent of everything, and you don't know, you don't
know. Just as someone swimming in sweet water has
no idea what it feels like to be thirsty.

MARIA. I don't want to repeat what I always say to you.

YERMA. Every day I want more and I hope less.

MARIA. That's not good.

YERMA. I'm going to end up thinking I'm my own son.

Night after night I go down to feed the oxen, which is
something I never used to do, because it's not woman's
work, but I do it now, and when I walk on the shed's
flagstones my footsteps sound to me like the footsteps
of a man.

MARIA. All God's creatures have their reasons to be.

YERMA. In spite of everything, don't hate me. You see
how I am.

MARIA. What about his sisters?

YERMA. Kill me and leave me to rot unburied if you
ever see me speak a word to them.

MARIA. What about your husband?

YERMA. It's three against one.

MARIA. What are they thinking?

YERMA. They imagine things. As people do when
they've got a bad conscience. They think there has to
be another man I'm after, and what they don't
understand is that even if there was someone in my
family our honour always comes first. They stand in my
way like boulders . . . But what they don't understand
is that, if I want, I can be water of a mountain torrent
that will wash them away.

One SISTER *comes in and goes out carrying a loaf of bread.*

MARIA. Whatever happens, I'm sure your husband still
loves you.

YERMA. My husband puts bread on the table and a roof
over my head.

MARIA. Dear God, the things you're going through and all you have to bear. Try to remember what Jesus went through as he was hanging on the cross!

They are standing by the door.

YERMA (*looking at the baby*). He's woken up.

MARIA. Soon he'll start to sing.

YERMA. He's got your eyes. Did you know that? Have you seen? (*Crying*) He's got your eyes!

YERMA *gently pushes* MARIA *out of the door, and she silently goes.* YERMA *is about to go to the door her husband went through.*

GIRL 2. Pssst!

YERMA (*turning back*). What is it?

GIRL 2. I was waiting for her to leave. My mother's waiting for you.

YERMA. Is she on her own?

GIRL 2. She's with two neighbours.

YERMA. Tell her to wait a minute.

GIRL 2. But are you coming? You're not afraid?

YERMA. I'm coming.

GIRL 2. Rather you than me!

YERMA. Tell them to wait, even if I come late!

VICTOR *enters.*

VICTOR. Is Juan in?

YERMA. Yes.

GIRL 2 (*conspiratorially*). I'll bring you the blouse then.

YERMA. When you can.

The GIRL *leaves.*

Sit down.

VICTOR. I'm best to stand.

YERMA (*calls out for her husband*). Juan!

VICTOR. I've come to say goodbye.

YERMA (*shivers a little, but returns to her state of apparent calm*). Are you going with your brothers?

VICTOR. That's what my father wants.

YERMA. He must be getting old.

VICTOR. Yes. He's getting on.

Pause.

YERMA. It's a good idea for you to move.

VICTOR. Everywhere's the same.

YERMA. No. I'd get right out of here.

VICTOR. It's all the same. The sheep are the same. They all have wool.

YERMA. That may be true for men, but for us women it's another story. I never heard a man eat an apple and say: 'These apples taste so good!' You just take what's yours without noticing the joy in it. All I can say about me and this place is that I have learnt to hate the water that comes from its wells.

VICTOR. Maybe.

The stage is now in a gentle twilight. Pause.

YERMA. Victor.

VICTOR. What?

YERMA. Why are you going? People like you here.

VICTOR. I behaved as I should.

YERMA. Oh yes. You were very correct. When you were still a boy you carried me once in your arms. Do you remember? We never know how things may turn out.

VICTOR. Everything changes.

YERMA. Some things don't change. Some things get bricked in behind walls and they can't change because no one can hear them.

VICTOR. That's true.

SISTER 2 *appears and slowly goes to the door where she stands lit by the light of the setting sun.*

YERMA. Because if they could suddenly get out and scream, they would scream so loud the sound would fill the world.

VICTOR. That wouldn't help. Water flows down its channel, sheep belong to the sheepfold, and the man belongs to the plough.

YERMA. What a shame I can't appreciate the wisdom of the old!

We hear the long melancholic sounds of the shepherd's conch shells.

VICTOR. They're bringing the flocks home.

JUAN (*entering*). Are you away now?

VICTOR. I want to reach the port before daybreak.

JUAN. Have you any complaint?

VICTOR. No. Not against you. You always paid on time.

JUAN (*to* YERMA). I bought his sheep.

YERMA. Really?

VICTOR (*to* YERMA). They're all yours.

YERMA. I didn't know that.

JUAN (*complacently*). That's what's happened.

VICTOR. Your husband will be so rich.

YERMA. Money comes to the hands of the man who works for it.

The SISTER *who was at the doorway goes inside.*

JUAN. We'll have nowhere to put so many sheep.

YERMA (*sombrely*). The earth is wide.

Pause.

JUAN. I'll walk you to the stream.

VICTOR. I wish this house all happiness.

He shakes YERMA *by the hand.*

YERMA. God hear you. Goodbye.

VICTOR *takes his leave, and then, in response to an imperceptible signal from* YERMA, *turns back.*

VICTOR. Did you say something?

YERMA (*charged with emotion*). I said goodbye.

VICTOR. Goodbye.

They go. YERMA *casts an anguished look at her hand, which has just touched* VICTOR's. *She heads rapidly to the left and takes a cloak.*

GIRL 2 (*quietly, putting up her hood*). Let's go.

YERMA. Let's go.

> *They go out cautiously. The stage is now almost dark.*
> SISTER 1 *enters with a candle that gives no more than its*
> *natural light. She goes to the back of the stage looking for*
> YERMA. *We hear the conch shells calling the sheep.*

SISTER 1 (*in a low voice*). Yerma!

> *Enter* SISTER 2. *They give each other a look and head for the*
> *door.*

SISTER 2 (*louder*). Yerma! (*She goes out.*)

SISTER 1 (*also going to the door, and calling out harshly*).
Yerma!

> *She goes out. We hear the conch shells and the horn of the*
> *shepherds calling their sheep. The stage is in almost total*
> *darkness.*

> *Curtain.*

ACT THREE

Scene One

The house belonging to DOLORES, *the wise woman and witch. Dawn is breaking.*

Enter YERMA *with* DOLORES *and two* OLD WOMEN.

DOLORES. You've been brave.

OLD WOMAN 1. Nothing as strong as the heart's desire.

OLD WOMAN 2. But it was too dark in the graveyard.

DOLORES. There's been so many times I've spoken
these prayers in the graveyard with women who
wanted children and they've all been afraid. Every
single one but you.

YERMA. I came to get a child. And I trust you.

DOLORES. You're right to. If I have ever lied may my
tongue be covered in ants like a corpse's. The last time
I did that prayer it was for a beggarwoman, who was
barren for longer than you, and her belly softened in
so beautiful a way that she had twins down there by
the river because they didn't give her time to get to a
house, and she herself brought them to me wrapped
up in a headscarf so I could sort them.

YERMA. And she could walk all the way from the river?

DOLORES. That's what she did. Her shoes and her
petticoats were soaked in blood. But her face was
shining.

YERMA. And there was nothing wrong with her?

DOLORES. What could go wrong? God is God.

YERMA. Of course. Nothing could happen. She just had to take hold of the wee things and wash them in living water. Animals lick their young, don't they? The idea doesn't disgust me at all. I think that new mothers must be lit up by a light inside them and that the babies sleep for hours and hours and hours just listening to this stream of warm milk that fills their breasts so the babies can suck and suck and take their pleasure until they don't need any more, till their heads drop back, have another wee drop my baby, and their faces and their chests are spattered with the white drops.

DOLORES. I assure you. You will have a son.

YERMA. I will have him because I have to. Or the world makes no sense. At times when I think that he will never never come it's like a wave of fire that comes up from my feet and burns everything up, so that the men who walk down the street and the bulls and the stones just look like bits of cotton wool. And I ask myself, what are they doing here?

OLD WOMAN 1. It's right and proper for a married woman to want a son, but if she doesn't have one, why go through all this agony? The most important thing is just to let life happen. I'm not criticising. You saw how I helped you do the prayers. But what do you expect to give your child? Can you give him a meadow? Can you give him happiness? Can you give him a throne of gold?

YERMA. I don't think about tomorrow. I think about today. You're an old old woman and life's like a book you finished reading years ago. I feel I have no freedom. I have thirst. I want to hold my son in my arms, that's the only way I can have peace. Listen to this, and don't get too upset by what I'm saying: even if I knew my son was really going to make me suffer and beat me even and drag me through the streets by the hair, his birth would still fill me with joy. Because it's better to be made to cry by a living man who beats us than be crying for a ghost that's been sitting on my heart for year after year.

OLD WOMAN 1. You're too young to listen to advice. But still, while you're waiting for the grace and mercy of God, you'd do better to take refuge in your husband's love.

YERMA. Oh God! You've just put your finger on my body's deepest wound.

DOLORES. You've got a good husband.

YERMA (*getting up*). Oh yes, he's good. He's very good. So what? I wish he were bad. No. He counts his sheep by day and he counts his money by night. And when he covers me, when he tries to inseminate me, he's just doing it out of duty and he's as cold as a corpse. And me, me who's always been disgusted by women on heat, and that moment . . . that moment I wish I were a mountain of fire.

DOLORES. Yerma!

YERMA. There's nothing indecent about me. Nothing unchaste. But I know where children come from. They come from a woman and a man. Oh, if only, if only I could have them alone!

DOLORES. Think about your husband. He must be suffering too.

YERMA. He doesn't suffer. The thing about him is he doesn't want a child.

OLD WOMAN 1. Don't say that!

YERMA. I can tell it from the way he looks at me. And because he doesn't want one, he can't give me one. He doesn't want one, he doesn't want one, yet he's the only way I can get one. Because of my honour and my family. He's the only way.

OLD WOMAN 1 (*afraid*). It'll soon be dawn. You should go home.

DOLORES. They'll be taking the flocks out very soon and you shouldn't be seen alone.

YERMA. I needed to get that off my chest. How often do I say the prayers?

DOLORES. The laurel prayer you say twice, and then at midday you say the prayer of Saint Anne. And then when you're pregnant you bring me the bushel of wheat you promised.

OLD WOMAN 1. The light is breaking over the mountain. Go.

DOLORES. They'll be opening their front doors now. You'll have to take the back path.

YERMA (*discouraged*). I don't know why I came!

DOLORES. Are you sorry you did?

YERMA. No.

DOLORES (*disturbed*). If you're afraid, I'll walk you down to the corner.

OLD WOMAN 1 (*anxious*). It'll be broad daylight before you get to your door.

We hear voices.

DOLORES. Listen! (*They listen.*)

OLD WOMAN 1. It's no one. Go with God.

YERMA *goes to the door and that moment someone knocks on it. The three women stand stock-still.*

DOLORES. Who is it?

VOICE. It's me.

YERMA. Open the door.

DOLORES *hesitates.*

I said open the door!

We hear mutterings. JUAN *and the two* SISTERS *appear.*

SISTER 2. There she is!

YERMA. Here I am!

JUAN. What are you doing in this place? If I could I'd shout out loud enough to wake the whole village so they could see where my house's honour has gone. But I have to stifle everything because you are my wife.

YERMA. If I could shout, I'd be shouting out too, so that even the dead could get up from their graves and see me clothed in all innocence.

JUAN. No! I can put up with everything but that! You are deceiving me, you weave around me your web of deceit and lies. And I'm a simple man, a straightforward man who works the earth, and I can't deal with your deviousness.

DOLORES. Juan!

JUAN. And not a word from you!

DOLORES (*fiercely*). Your wife has done nothing wrong.

JUAN. She's been undermining me since the day we got married. She's got two needles for eyes and she sticks them into me. She never sleeps at night. She stays awake all the time staring at me and infecting my bedroom with her misery.

YERMA. Shut up!

JUAN. I can't stand it any more. You'd have to be made out of stone to put up with a woman who wants to stick her fingers right into your heart and who goes out into the street at night looking for what? Tell me! Looking for what? The streets are full of men. And you don't go out the door to pick flowers.

YERMA. I won't let you say one word more. You imagine that you and your people are the only ones who are honourable, and you ignore the fact that my family has never had to hide anything from anybody. Come here. Come up to me and smell my clothes, come here and do it! And see if you notice any smell that is not yours, that does not belong to your body. You're stripping me naked in the middle of the village square and spitting on me. I know I'm your wife and you have the right to do whatever you want, but don't you dare impute a man's name on my breasts.

JUAN. It's not something I do. It's something you do with your behaviour, and the people are beginning to say so openly. When I come up to a group of people, they all fall silent; when I go to weigh the flour, they all fall silent; and even at night in the fields, when I wake up, it seems to me the branches of the trees are falling silent too.

YERMA. I know there's a bad wind blowing and it's stirring up the wheat on the threshing floor. And is the wheat good? Or is it rotten? You should look and see.

JUAN. What I want to know is why a woman should be out looking for something at all hours of the night.

YERMA (*embracing her husband with a sudden impulse*). I'm looking for you. I am looking for you. It's you I'm looking for day and night without finding any shade in which to breathe. It's your blood and your protection I desire.

JUAN. Get away from me.

YERMA. Don't drive me away. Find a way to love me.

JUAN. Leave me alone!

YERMA. Look at me. I am abandoned and alone. As if the moon had to look for herself in the sky. Look at me! (*She looks at him.*)

JUAN (*looks at her then abruptly withdraws his gaze*). Just leave me alone!

DOLORES. Juan!

YERMA *falls to the ground.*

YERMA (*loudly*). When I went out to look for flowers I came slap up against a stone wall. Ay! Ay! And over and over again I keep banging my head against it! And I can't stop!

JUAN. Be quiet. Let's go home.

DOLORES. Oh my god!

YERMA (*shouting*). I curse the mother who gave me this wish to have children! I curse my desire so deep in my blood I keep searching for my children and can never find them!

JUAN. I said be quiet!

DOLORES. There are people coming! Keep your voices down!

YERMA. I don't care if people come. Let my voice at least be free, now I am entering the darkest point of this well. (*She gets up.*) Let this beautiful thing at least leave my body and fill the air.

We hear voices.

DOLORES. They're going to walk past here.

JUAN. Silence.

YERMA. It's that. It's that. Silence. Don't you worry.

JUAN. Home. Now!

YERMA. That's it! That's it! And it's no use wringing my hands! It's one thing to wish with the head . . .

JUAN. Be quiet!

YERMA (*in a low voice*). It's one thing to wish with the head but whether the body actually responds is something else altogether. This accursed body. What is written is written, and I'm not going to fight against

the waves of the sea. I can't. May my mouth stay
soundless and dumb! (*She leaves.*)

Curtain.

Final Scene

*Outside a hermitage on the high mountain. Downstage, some
cartwheels and blankets form a rough shelter, where* YERMA *sits.
The* WOMEN *come in with offerings. They are barefoot. Also on
stage is the cheerful* PAGAN OLD WOMAN *of the first act.*

A song behind the closed curtain:

> When you were single, my lovely
> We never could meet.
> But now that you're married, my lovely
> Your body I'll greet.
> When the clocks strike twelve, my lovely,
> I will strip you bare.
> Join the pilgrims, my lovely,
> And I'll meet you there.

OLD WOMAN (*sarcastically*). You sure you've drunk the
holy water?

WOMAN 1. Yes.

OLD WOMAN. And next you've got to see the saint.

WOMAN 2. We believe in his power.

OLD WOMAN. So you come here to ask the saint for
children. And all that happens is that every year more
and more single men come too. It's a miracle. (*She
laughs.*)

WOMAN 1. If you don't believe in it, why do you come?

OLD WOMAN. To watch. I love to watch. And take
care of my son. Last year two men knifed each other
over some barren wife and I want to be on guard. And
in the end I come because I want to.

WOMAN 1. God forgive you! (*They go in.*)

OLD WOMAN (*sarcastically*). And God forgive you and
all.

She goes. Enter MARIA *with* GIRL 1.

GIRL 1. And did she come?

MARIA. Their cart's over there. I had to work hard to
get them to come. She's spent the whole of the last
month just sitting. Just sitting in her chair. I'm
frightened of her. She's got an idea in her head. I
don't know what it is. But it's obvious it's something
wicked.

GIRL 1. I came with my sister. She's been coming for
eight years. And nothing.

MARIA. The one who's meant to have children will have
them.

GIRL 1. That's what I say.

We hear voices.

MARIA. I never liked this festival. Let's go to the
threshing floors, where the people are.

GIRL 1. Last year when it got dark, some boys got hold
of my sister's breasts.

MARIA. For miles all around all you hear are dirty words.

GIRL 1. I saw forty barrels of wine just round the back
of the church . . . Forty! I counted them.

MARIA. There's crowds and crowds of men coming
from all around.

We hear voices. YERMA *comes in with* WOMEN *going to
the church. Their feet are bare and they carry fluted candles.
Night begins to fall.*

YERMA.
Lord, may the rose come in flower
And may I not be left in darkness.

WOMAN 2.
Lord, may the yellow rose flower
On her fading yellow flesh.

YERMA.
Lord, in the belly of your servant
Light the earth's dark flame.

CHORUS OF WOMEN.
Lord, may the rose come in flower
And may I not be left in darkness.

They kneel.

YERMA.
Heaven has gardens
Where roses grow in joy
Among all the flowers
The miraculous rose.
Like a guardian archangel
Or a ray of light from the dawn.
Its eyes are like agonies
Its wings are like storms.

Its sap of warm milk
Gives life to its leaves.
Its warm drops are falling
To moisten the faces
Of the tranquil stars.
O Lord, may the yellow rose flower
On my fading flesh.

They get up.

WOMAN 2.

Lord, calm with your soft hand
The burning flames of her cheek.

YERMA.

Listen to this pilgrim
Travelling your holy path
Forgive all her great sins.
And open your rose
Though it has a thousand thorns.

CHORUS.

Lord, may the rose come in flower
And may I not be left in darkness.

YERMA.

On my fading flesh
The miraculous rose.

They go in.

GIRLS run on with long ribbons from the left, cross the stage, and run off again.

Then another three GIRLS enter from the right, also cross, and rush off again. There's a crescendo of voices, with the sounds of little bells and tambourines. High up on the stage seven GIRLS appear, waving their ribbons to the left. The noise grows louder and two folkloric figures enter, one representing the MALE *and the other the* FEMALE. *They wear huge masks. The* MALE *carries a bull's horns in his hand. They are in no way grotesque, but of great beauty and communicate a sense of belonging to the ancient earth. The* FEMALE *shakes a collar of bells. The back of the stage fills up with a* CROWD *of people who shout and pass comments on the dance. Darkness is falling.*

BOY. The devil and his wife! The devil and his wife!

FEMALE.
In the river of the mountain
The sad wife was bathing.
Up her body went crawling
Sad snails of the water.
The sand on the riverbank
And the breezes of the mountain
Set fire to her laughter
And made her shoulders shake and shiver.
Oh, she was naked
She was very very naked
The sad wife in the water!

BOY. Oh, how sad she was! How sad!

MAN 1.
How dead withered flower
In the wind and the water!

MAN 2.
Tell the one who waits!

MAN 1.
Tell the one who's awaiting!

MAN 2.
> Her with the dry belly
> And the broken colour!

FEMALE.
> When night comes I'll tell him
> Under the clear dark night of sky
> The night when the dry women gather
> That's when I tear my skirt open.

CHORUS.
> And at once the night falls!
> The dark night was coming!
> Look how black and dark it is getting
> By the banks of the river in the mountain.

Guitars start to play.

MALE (*getting up and starting to wave his horns*).
> How pale and wan is the lonely wife
> How sad she is among the dead flowers!
> But soon you will open your scarlet flowers
> When the male unfolds his dark cloak.

He comes closer.

> If you come to the church
> To ask for your belly to ripen
> Don't wear a veil of mourning
> But a blouse of fine silk
> Go alone behind the walls
> Under the shade of the fig trees
> And bear the weight of my earth body
> From dusk till day's dawning.
> Oh, how the moon shines

How bright the sun is shining!
And look how her hips are swaying.

FEMALE.

Crown her with flowers
Adorn her breasts with pure gold!

MALE.

Seven times was she moaning
In her joy and her delight
Seven times seven was there joining
Bright day and dark night.

MAN 1.

And the horn slips inside her!

MAN 2.

With the rose and the dance.

MAN 1.

Oh, how the wife is swaying!

MALE.

The male always rules
In this pilgrimage.
The husbands are bulls
And the male always governs,
And the pilgrims are flowers
For the men who can pick them.

BOY.

Let the air come inside her!

MAN 2.

Nail her with the branch!

MALE.

Come and see the pale woman
Now she's swimming in the fire.

MAN 1.

She's swaying like a reed.

BOY.

She's opening like a flower.

MEN.

Young girls should look elsewhere!

MALE.

The woman's body burns
The woman's body shines
And honour is scattered like ashes.

They go off dancing to the sound of handclaps and music. They are singing.

There are gardens in the sky
With rosebushes of joy
And among them all
The miracle of the rose.

Two GIRLS *pass across the stage again, shrieking. Enter the cheerful* PAGAN OLD WOMAN.

OLD WOMAN. Who'll make more noise, I wonder. Will it be him or her, I wonder. Will we get any sleep, I wonder.

Enter YERMA.

You?

YERMA *is depressed. She says nothing.*

What are you doing here?

YERMA. I don't know.

OLD WOMAN. You don't believe in it? What about your husband?

YERMA *shows her exhaustion. She looks like someone whose mind is totally oppressed by some idea she cannot shift.*

YERMA. He's over there.

OLD WOMAN. What's he doing?

YERMA. Drinking. (*Pause. She takes her head in her hands and starts to cry.*)

OLD WOMAN. Less tears. More courage. I didn't want to say anything to you before. But I will now.

YERMA. What can you tell me that I don't know already!

OLD WOMAN. The one thing you can't go on ignoring. The thing that shouts from the rooftops. It's your husband who's to blame. Can you hear that? It's true what I'm saying. Or cut off both my hands. Neither his father, his grandfather or his great grandfather ever held themselves like real men. It's been a kind of miracle they've ever had children. They're made out of spit. But not your people. You have got brothers and cousins for miles all around. Look how great a curse has fallen on your beauty!

YERMA. Yes. A curse. A pool of poison in the fields.

OLD WOMAN. But you have legs. Use them. Walk out your house.

YERMA. Walk out?

OLD WOMAN. When I saw you in the pilgrimage my heart missed a beat. This is where the women come to meet new men and that's the Saint's miracle. My son's sitting behind the church waiting for me. My house

needs a woman. Go with him and the three of us will
live together. My son has real blood in his veins. Like
me. If you come into my house it still smells of babies.
The ash of your mattress will turn into bread and salt
for your children. Come. Don't listen to what people
say. As for your husband, I've got enough knives and
castrating irons in my house to make sure he doesn't
even dare cross the street.

YERMA. Quiet! Don't say another word! I could never
do that. Do you imagine I could ever know another
man? What do you think of my honour? Water cannot
flow uphill. The moon cannot come out at midday.
Go away. I'll keep following the path I'm on. Did you
really imagine that I could go off with another man?
That like a slave I would go begging for what's already
mine? Know me better. Never talk to me again.

OLD WOMAN. Someone who's thirsty is grateful for
water.

YERMA. I'm like a dried-up field where there's room for
a thousand pairs of oxen. And what you offer me is a
small glass of water from the well. Mine is a grief that
does not reside in flesh.

OLD WOMAN (*fiercely*). Then go on like this. It's what
you choose. Like thistles on a desert. Withered.
Barren.

YERMA (*fiercely*). Yes. Barren. I know that. Barren. You
don't have to rub my face in it. Don't be like one of
those boys that take pleasure in the death agony of
some little creature he's been tormenting. Since I got
married I've been going round and round this word,

but this is the first time I've heard it spoken, the first time anyone has ever said it to my face. The first time I see that it is true.

OLD WOMAN. I don't have any sympathy for you. None at all. I'll find my son another woman.

She goes. We hear a distant song sung by the pilgrims.
YERMA goes to the cart and JUAN appears from behind it.

YERMA. Were you there?

JUAN. I was there.

YERMA. Were you listening?

JUAN. I was listening.

YERMA. And did you hear?

JUAN. Every word.

YERMA. Leave me alone and join the singing. (*She sits on some blankets.*)

JUAN. And now it's time I spoke.

YERMA. Then speak!

JUAN. And that I complain.

YERMA. Why?

JUAN. My throat is choked in bitterness.

YERMA. And it eats away my bones.

JUAN. I'm utterly beyond being able to deal with this endless lament for dark things, things outside life, things that only live in the air.

YERMA (*with total astonishment*). Outside life? Is that what you're saying? In the air?

JUAN. Things which have happened and which have nothing to do with either of us.

YERMA (*violently*). Go on! Go on!

JUAN. Things that don't matter to me. Do you hear me? Things that don't matter to me. I need to tell you. What matters to me is what I can hold in my hands. What I can see with my own eyes.

YERMA (*getting on to her knees in desperation*). Yes. Yes. That's what I needed to hear you speak. When the truth is locked inside, you can't see it, but how big it becomes, how much it matters when it is spoken out and lives in the open! And you think it doesn't matter! Now I've heard you say it!

JUAN (*getting close to her*). Think about it. That's how it has to be. Listen to me.

He embraces her to help her on her feet.

Many women would be so happy to live the way you do. Life is sweeter without children. I'm so happy not to have any. And we are not to blame.

YERMA. So what are you looking for in me?

JUAN. Your self.

YERMA (*excited*). Yes. That. You were looking for a home, peace and quiet, and a wife. But nothing else. Is it true what I'm saying?

JUAN. It's true. As everything.

YERMA. And what about the rest? What about your son?

JUAN (*angrily*). Didn't you hear me? I said it doesn't matter! Don't ask any more of me! Have I got to shout it in your ear to make you understand. To see if for just this once you could be at peace!

YERMA. And you've never thought about it when you've seen me desiring it?

JUAN. Never.

They are both on the ground.

YERMA. And there's no use me hoping?

JUAN. No.

YERMA. And what about you?

JUAN. Nothing. Get used to it!

YERMA. Barren!

JUAN. And living in peace. You with me, calmly, pleasantly. Embrace me! (*He embraces her.*)

YERMA. What do you want?

JUAN. You. You're so beautiful under the moon.

YERMA. You're looking at me like you're looking at a chicken. Or a sheep.

JUAN. Kiss me . . . Like this.

YERMA. No. Never. Never.

YERMA *lets out a cry and compresses her husband's neck. He falls backwards.* YERMA *continues to strangle him until he has died. The pilgrim's chorus starts to sing.*

Barren. Barren. Barren. But at least I know for sure. Now I absolutely know it for sure. And alone.

She gets up. PEOPLE *start to arrive.*

Now I can rest without ever having to wake up
startled, wondering if there is new life in my blood.
With a body barren for ever. What do you want to
know? Keep away from me. I have killed my son. I
have killed my own son!

A CROWD *gather who stay stock-still upstage. We hear the
pilgrim's chorus.*

Curtain.